LONELY PLANET

BY STEVEN DIETZ

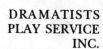

★

**DRAMATISTS
PLAY SERVICE
INC.**

This play was written for, and is dedicated to,
Michael Winters and Larry Ballard.

LONELY PLANET received its premiere at Northlight Theatre (Russell Vandenbroucke, Artistic Director), in Evanston, Illinois, on January 20th, 1993. It was directed by Steven Dietz; the set design was by James Dardenne; the costume design was by Gayland Spalding; the lighting design was by Rita Pietraszek; the sound design was by David Zerlin and the stage manager was Patty Lyons. The cast was as follows:

JODY..William Brown
CARL ....Phil Ridarelli

LONELY PLANET was produced by A Contemporary Theatre (Jeff Steitzer, Artistic Director) in Seattle, Washington, on July 8, 1993. It was directed by Steven Dietz; the set design was by Scott Weldin; the costume design was by Carolyn Keim; the lighting design was by Rick Paulsen; the dramaturg was Steven E. Alter and the stage manager was Craig Weindling. The cast was as follows:

JODY.. Michael Winters
CARL ....Laurence Ballard

LONELY PLANET was produced by The Barrow Group (Seth Barrish, Artistic Director), in New York City, in February, 1994. It was directed by Leonard Foglia; the set design was by Michael McGarty; the costume design was by Markas Henry; the lighting design was by Howard Werner; the sound design was by One Dream and the stage manager was Deborah Heimann. The cast was as follows:

JODY..Mark Shannon
CARL .... Denis O'Hare

ACKNOWLEDGMENT

The author wishes to thank Kevin Kling, Jim Stowell, the Playwrights' Center in Minneapolis and Susan Booth for their contributions to the development of this play.

And, a special note of gratitude for TXT, who gave me my first Peters Projection Map — and thereby made this play possible.

CHARACTERS

JODY, a man in his forties.
CARL, a man in his early thirties.

TIME

The present.

PLACE

Jody's Maps, a small map store on the oldest street in an American city.

We will leave some traces, for we are people and not cities.

— Ionesco, *The Chairs*

LONELY PLANET

ACT ONE

Scene 1

In a shaft of light we see a simple, wooden chair. Nothing else. Jody stands, looking at the chair for a long time. Then, he looks at the audience.

JODY.   One day I saw a chair here. I had no idea where it had come from. I looked at it. I sat in it. *(He sits, pause.)* A chair. Nothing else. *(Lights expand to reveal the store: Jody's Maps. There are numerous maps on the walls, globes on pedestals, travel books in wooden cases, rolled up maps poking out of bins. A small counter with an old, vintage cash register. A map table with drawers. A water cooler. A front door which contains several small window panes. Featured prominently is a huge photo of planet Earth as seen from space. Morning. A sign hanging in the window tells customers that the store is "Closed." Carl enters, quickly. He stops and stands in the center of the room.)*

CARL.   Can I just say this? Can I just say this one thing?

JODY.   Certainly.

CARL.   Everyone is boring. How did this happen? *When* did this happen? At some imperceptible moment everyone became absolutely shuffle-your-feet, stare-out-the-window *boring*. I try, okay? I do my part. I strike things up. I toss out words to grease the conversation. But these people, these people at the bus or the market or the newsstand, these people bore me. Not just a little. They bore me a lot. I'm sure they all came from good families, but over time they've lost what small part of them was ever of interest to anyone. They are even sort of hard to *see*.

JODY. Carl?

CARL. Yes?

JODY. Where did this chair come from?

CARL. I know. I've read the books. I can imagine people in their underwear. That helps, for a while. Then their underwear starts to bore me. So, I imagine them without their underwear, and then their embarrassment bores me. So, I imagine them in my underwear and that's moderately exciting, until they roll over, drop ashes on my pillow and say "I heard this joke at the cash machine today. You're gonna love it. It'll kill you." And they're right. It does. The yawn begins in my groin and stops at their eyes. I watch shadows fill the room like a cancer.

JODY. Carl —

CARL. So, finally, I try to imagine these people as someone else and soon *that* person bores me, and I imagine that person as someone else and *they* bore me, and so on and so on until I've imagined them all into something so small and distant and insignificant that there is nothing left but me standing alone at the bus, alone at the market, alone at the newsstand — reading an article about the tidal wave of boredom that is sweeping the nation. And, naturally, the article bores me. All I'm saying is this: Don't step out your door in the morning until you've thought of something interesting to say.

JODY. Carl, let me ask you something —

CARL. Not now, Jody. I've got things to do. *(Carl exits. Silence. Jody rises from the chair and moves to the counter. He presses a key on the old cash register and the cash drawer opens. From the drawer he takes a wrapped toothpick. Closes the drawer. Unwraps the toothpick. Stands in his shop. Stares at the huge photo of planet Earth. Picks at his teeth with pleasure. It's a lovely, quiet morning. Carl enters, calmly.)* I'm much better now. Thanks. Any good dreams?

JODY. Not now, Carl.

CARL. Your sign says you're closed. Are you closed?

JODY. No, Carl. I'm open. *(Jody moves to the sign in the door.)*

CARL. You should turn it. You should adjust it to reflect accuracy. This is twice now, Jody. This is twice I've noticed this. *(Jody turns the sign to read "Open.")*

JODY. There.

CARL. You asked about the chair.

JODY. I did.

CARL. A good chair, isn't it? A strong chair.

JODY. I don't need a chair, Carl. This shop is getting too small as it is.

CARL. A person could sit in it.

JODY. You know me, Carl. I am perpetually fighting clutter.

CARL. A person could peruse a map. A person could plan a trip, an adventure —

JODY. Carl?

CARL. Yes.

JODY. We need to play our game.

CARL. What game is that, Jody?

JODY. Our game, Carl. The game we play.

CARL. Names of child stars who were miserable in later life?

JODY. No.

CARL. A different game?

JODY. Yes.

CARL. Oh. *(Silence.)*

JODY. Well? *(Silence.)*

CARL. The game where we tell the truth.

JODY. Yes.

CARL. Okay. *(Silence.)*

JODY. Well? *(Silence.)*

CARL. Jody?

JODY. What?

CARL. I can't play our game, yet. I'd prefer to lie a little longer.

JODY. That's your choice, Carl.

CARL. I got the chair at an auction.

JODY. Did you?

CARL. Yes. I did very well. I got it for a song.

JODY. That's wonderful.

CARL. Yes. You should have come with. You'd have loved it.

11

JODY. Maybe next time.

CARL. You need to get out more.

JODY. So you've told me. Anything else?

CARL. Actually, I found it. Stroke of luck. I was walking to the newsstand — and there it was, abandoned, just lying in the alley. So, now it's mine, Jody — ours.

JODY. I see.

CARL. A good chair, isn't it?

JODY. Yes.

CARL. Did you sit in it?

JODY. Yes, I did.

CARL. Good.

JODY. Anything else?

CARL. Any good dreams?

JODY. Carl.

CARL. What?

JODY. Anything *else? (Silence.)*

CARL. No, I think that's all for now. *(Jody stares at him.)*

JODY. O.K. *(Carl sits and watches Jody, expectantly.)* I am a fireman. *(Carl smiles.)* Well, not really. What happened was I had bought this fireman's shirt — dark blue, you know, with the patch, the real McCoy — I had bought this shirt at a second hand store — some childhood dream come home to roost, something, who knows, but anyway — now I'm wearing it. I am walking down the street, wearing my fireman's shirt, and a tragedy strikes. I'm not sure what the tragedy is, actually. The dream never lets me see the actual tragedy. What I do see, though, is all these people rushing up to me for help. They need me to do C.P.R. They need me to dash into burning buildings. They need me to climb ladders and haul babies out of smoke. And I keep saying: "Look, it's just a *shirt.* I bought it second-hand. You've got the wrong person." But, they are relentless. They demand I help them. They won't take no for an answer. And I just keep saying: "You've got the wrong person. I'm not a fireman. I own a map store. I don't have any of the skills that you —" *(Stops.)*

CARL. What?

JODY. I just remembered something.

CARL. What?

JODY. You are there.

CARL. I am?

JODY. Yes. And I say: "Tell them, Carl. Tell them I'm not a fireman. Tell them I can't save them."

CARL. And what do I do?

JODY. You hand me a ladder and say: "Jody, don't let us down."

CARL. I was kidding, Jody. I was just —

JODY. No one is kidding in dreams. No one is just casually chatting.

CARL. So, what do you do?

JODY. I climb the ladder toward the fire, my ax in my hand. I hear their screams in my ears. I feel the heat on my face. *(Pause.)* Then, I wake up.

CARL. Thank god.

JODY. You were no help, Carl.

CARL. I'm sorry.

JODY. And I don't need a chair.

CARL. Fine. I'll take it home with me.

JODY. Good.

CARL. What time is it?

JODY. Nine fifteen.

CARL. Oh, my god. *(Rushes to the door.)* I'm late, Jody. I had an eight thirty meeting and I totally — oh, god. I'll see you, Jody. I'll call you later — *(Carl is gone. Jody, unfazed, goes to the water cooler. Draws a paper cup of water. He stands in his shop, drinking water and watching the door. He looks at his watch, smiles. Then, he moves to the door and opens it — just as Carl reenters.)*

JODY. Hello, Carl.

CARL. Jody.

JODY. Meeting go well?

CARL. I was lying, Jody.

JODY. I know that.

CARL. I wanted to dash out and leave the chair behind.

JODY. I know that.

CARL. But I've rethought things.

JODY. You have? *(Carl sets the chair down in front of Jody.)*

CARL. Happy Birthday, Jody! *(Hugs him.)* You're a great friend and though it's hard to shop for the man who has everything, I saw this — *(Indicates the chair.)* — and, well —

JODY. Thank you, Carl.

CARL. So, you'll take it?

JODY. Yes.

CARL. You'll take the chair?

JODY. Yes.

CARL. It's not really your birthday, is it?

JODY. No, Carl.

CARL. Thank god, I don't have a thing to give you.

JODY. I'll take the chair, Carl.

CARL. Great.

JODY. Are you happy now?

CARL. I'm happy, take my picture.

JODY. *(Takes chair.)* I'm going to Goodwill tomorrow. I'll take it with me. Someone will put it to good use.

CARL. *(Grabs chair back from Jody.)* Actually, truth be told, I bought it for my apartment.

JODY. You live in a shoe box, Carl. You've got no room for —

CARL. I'm knocking out a wall. This chair will be stunning. It will be the missing link in my — you know — my decorating —

JODY. Your decorating what?

CARL. My —

JODY. Yes?

CARL. *Scheme.* My decorating *scheme.*

JODY. Can we play our game now, Carl?

CARL. *(Sharp.)* I don't want it taken to Goodwill. I've got to go. *(Carl picks up the chair.)*

JODY. Where are you going?

CARL. I HAVE PLANTS TO WATER. Have a good day, Jody. Hope business picks up.

JODY. Carl —

CARL. Bye. *(Carl leaves, taking the chair with him. Jody stares at the door for a moment, then turns and talks to the audience.)*

JODY.   This is the way things go with Carl. I've probably known him as long as anyone. He was one of my first customers here. Browsed for two hours and then went home with the Caribbean. Since then, he's been a fixture. Depending on which day you ask him, what Carl does for a living is either water plants for corporations, work as an art restorer at the museum, run an auto glass shop, write for a disreputable tabloid, or work as a bartender. He has the energy of eight and the patience of none. You can never pin him down. Carl is a constant reminder of what I love about maps: they are *fixed objects*. They have been called "surrogates of space." They attempt to make order and reduce our reliance on hypotheses. They are a picture of what's known. *(Carl tiptoes in, still carrying the chair.)*
CARL.   Am I interrupting?
JODY.   No.
CARL.   Bobby's dead, Jody. *(Pause.)* The memorial is Thursday. *(Carl walks into the room and sets the chair down. He looks up at Jody.)* Jody.
JODY.   *(Soft.)* What?
CARL.   Don't let us down.

Scene 2

Noon. The store is "Open." Three dozen chairs of all varieties have been placed around the room. For a long while, we stare at the room. Then, we hear voices.

VOICE OF CARL.   *(From behind the map table.)* I AM THE BASTARD SON OF RICHARD NIXON AND I SHALL RULE THE WORLD!
VOICE OF JODY.   *(From behind the counter.)* ADVANCE THEN, IF YOU DARE! *(Jody and Carl leap up from their hiding places and scream: AAAHHH! They race toward each other at the center of the room. They each hold long, rolled-up maps wrapped in plastic — and they are in the midst of a playfully vicious duel, using their maps as swords. The following lines happen during the*

fighting.)

JODY.   Your lies have gone too far, they have jeopardized our fair kingdom and it is the will of the citizenry that you must die!

CARL.   I bow not to your authority. I hear not your cries. History shall be my judge and jury! I recognize only the Opinion Polls of the Most High.

JODY.   Renounce it all, oh foundling son of a most derelict tapeworm! You must this day renounce it all!

CARL.   Never, I say! Never!

JODY.   You must renounce your rutting father and his rotting legacy!

CARL.   'Tis a hero of whom you speak! Father Dick is a man of destiny, and 'tis I will fan the fire and fervor of his famous flame forever! *(A standoff.)*

JODY.   Fie, then, bastard boy. Prepare to meet thy maker.

CARL.   And at whose hand shall this appeasement be enacted?

JODY.   Why by my very hand, and this noble — *(Checks the end of the map/sword.)* Australian weapon of death!

CARL.   The gods laugh at thy piteous, pixiesh posturing. *(Carl spits. Jody spits back. Carl spits. Jody spits back.)* For 'tis I, knave, who hold the weapon which shall open thy torso and send thy wretched soul to hell's gaping maw.

JODY.   And pray, what weapon is that, sir?

CARL.   *(Under his breath.)* Just a second. *(He, too, reads the label on the end of his map/sword.)* Aha!

JODY.   What, sir? Do tell thy weapon's name. *(Pause, then Carl holds the map/sword high, triumphantly.)*

CARL.   CHINA! *(More dueling. Ad-libs. Some swords/maps may be dropped, and others picked up from the bins in the store. Finally, Jody is without a sword and is lying back over the counter. Carl is ready to finish him off. Under his breath.)* Beg for mercy.

JODY.   *(Also under his breath.)* What?

CARL.   *(Under his breath.)* Beg for mercy.

JODY.   *(Full voice.)* I beg of you, sir, MERCY.

CARL.   Beg not to me, quivering cur. Beg thy pagan gods to speed thy fate. *(Lifts map/sword high over his head.)* Let his-

tory note whom here was smote:
>   T'was the rightful heir of Dick Nixon
>   who did thy unworthy banner of flesh unfurl,
>   and with one great longitudinal thrust
>   did send thee from this world —

(As Carl begins his final thrust, the phone rings.) Shit. *(Jody answers the phone.)*

JODY.   Jody's Maps. *(Pause.)* Just a second. *(Jody hands the phone to Carl.)* For thee.

CARL.   What news?

JODY.   I know not.

CARL.   *(Into phone.)* Yes? *(Jody crosses the room to get a drink of water. He also picks up some of the strewn maps. Carl turns upstage with the phone, so we do not hear his conversation. After a moment, he hangs up the phone and heads for the door.)*

JODY.   What is it, Carl?

CARL.   I'm wanted at the museum. There is art to be restored.

JODY.   I see. *(Carl gets to the door.)* What kind of art?

CARL.   *(Stops.)* Pardon?

JODY.   What kind of art, Carl? What kind of art is in need of restoring today? *(Silence.)*

CARL.   Umm …

JODY.   Yes?

CARL.   *Old* art. Some very … old art needs restoring today.

JODY.   Which art, Carl? American, European, African? The Gaugin, the Rauschenberg, the Hopper? What kind of —

CARL.   The Hopper. It's the Hopper, Jody.

JODY.   Which Hopper?

CARL.   The one of his mother.

JODY.   That's not Hopper, Carl.

CARL.   No, of course not. The other one. The one, we've seen it together, Jody, the one with the clown and the general and the worker and the society couple. And the lanterns.

JODY.   "Soir Bleu."

CARL.   Yes, you see. And the woman with the cheeks, the rouged cheeks, red like meat, standing behind them all, looking down on them. "Soir Bleu."

JODY. Blue Night.

CARL. Yes.

JODY. And it is being restored?

CARL. Most definitely.

JODY. I see. *(Carl starts off again.)* What is being done?

CARL. *(Stops.)* The clown is, his, uh, face is falling. It is falling, sinking down into his costume. His white face. We must lift it up.

JODY. Lift it up?

CARL. Yes. And the woman, she is, uh, cracking. Her, uh, red cheeks are cracking and there is, uh, another woman, another woman behind her who is peeking through — and we can't have this, Jody, it would be wrong, it would be criminal, to allow this other woman, this *painted over woman* to get back into the picture. We must keep her out. She does not belong.

JODY. Who is this other woman?

CARL. We don't know her name, Jody. We don't know everything.

JODY. How do you know she doesn't belong?

CARL. Because she is *behind the paint*. She is trying to butt in, trying to crash the painting because she is the one with the answer to the riddle.

JODY. What riddle?

CARL. The riddle of the painting. Who are these people, why are they gathered? Who is the woman, who is she there to see, to whom is she about to speak?

JODY. And the woman behind the painting knows these things?

CARL. This and more. She's clever, Jody. She sleeps with her eyes open and always knows where you're parked. We must cover her back up. She must not give the answers.

JODY. Why, Carl?

CARL. Because, the painting *is* the questions. That's what it *is*. Without that, it's just cloth that's giving a frame a job.

JODY. I see.

CARL. I hoped you would.

JODY. You're not going to restore art, are you, Carl?

CARL. *(Direct.)* No.

JODY. You're on your way to get more chairs.

CARL. Three of them. *(Silence. Jody stands. During the following he takes a few chairs which are in the middle of the room — and adds them to stacks in the corners of the room.)* Is it still all right for me to store them here, Jody? This is the largest room I know of. You know I'd keep them at my place, you know that — but it's so tiny and there's, well, there's just no — *(Pause.)* Are they in the way, Jody?

JODY. *Yes.*

CARL. Be honest with me.

JODY. More honest than yes?

CARL. I don't think you —

JODY. They are *terribly* in the way. They block aisles. Customers trip over them. The first few were fine, Carl, they really were, but this is too much now. They are horribly, disastrously IN THE WAY. *(Pause.)* Is that clear?

CARL. Yes.

JODY. Good.

CARL. I'm glad we can be direct.

JODY. *Get rid of them, Carl. (Silence. Carl turns and looks at the chairs. Then, he turns back to Jody.)*

CARL. I'd known Bobby since I was five. It was the first day of kindergarten and I was playing on the swings before the first bell rang. A kid I'd never seen before walked up and started swinging right next to me. When the bell rang, we stopped swinging and started for the door. He grabbed the hood of my coat and said "What's your name?" I said Carl. He said "I'm Bobby." I said hi. He said "You want to be best friends?" I said okay. Then we went inside and became best friends for twenty-five years.

I think everything good is attained through simplicity. I think that's why when you're all fucked up they say you have a complex. *(Silence. Carl goes to the door. Opens it.)*

JODY. I'll see you tomorrow, Carl.

CARL. You will. *(Carl leaves. Jody goes to the closed door and stares out the glass. Then, he pulls the shade closed. He locks the*

door. He turns the sign from "Open" to "Closed." He turns to the audience. As Jody speaks, the lights in the room gradually shift from noon ... to dusk ... to night.)

JODY.   Any talk of maps ultimately comes around to one very specific, lingering issue: The Greenland Problem. *(He indicates a large Mercator Projection World Map on the wall.)*

Now, you may know this, but Greenland is actually about the size of Mexico. However, on the well known Mercator projection map — the one hanging in front of your classrooms in grade school — Greenland appears to be roughly the size of South America and twice the size of China. Clearly a world power to be reckoned with, if it were, you know, habitable.

The Mercator map also shows most of the earth's land mass to be in what we consider the "north," when, in fact, the "south" is more than double the size of the north. Scandinavia seems to dwarf India, though India is three times as large. And the old Soviet states appear to be twice the size of the entire African continent. In reality they are smaller. Smaller by, oh, about four million square miles.

A map maker takes a messy round world and puts it neat and flat on the wall in front of you. And to do this, a map maker must decide which distortions, which faulty perceptions he can live with — to achieve a map which suits his purposes. He must commit to viewing it from only one angle.

The Mercator map, developed in Germany in 1569, was a great aid to navigators since, for the first time, all lines of longitude ran perpendicular to the equator — or straight up to the top of the map — rather than converging toward the poles. This meant that all the lines of longitude and latitude intersected at right angles — and this meant that, for the *first time*, a sailor could draw a straight line between two fixed points on the map and steer a constant course between them. The map had accounted for the curve of the earth — the sailor did not have to.

To accomplish this, Mercator had to accept a distortion: the parallel lines of latitude would have to be spaced progressively further apart as they moved away from the equator.

This, in turn, would progressively distort the sizes and shapes of land masses — from zero distortion at the equator, to absolute distortion at the poles ... the Greenland Problem.

Mercator was a brilliant man. He freed the art of cartography from superstition, from the weight of medieval misconceptions. And his map revolutionized global navigation. He never intended it as a tool to teach the sizes and shapes of countries. He never intended to make Greenland a global behemoth. *(He points at Mercator map.)*

But, nearly four hundred and fifty years after Mercator, we still think the earth looks like this. It doesn't. It never has. But we've come to accept the distortion as fact. We've learned to see the world from this angle.

I like this map. I sell this map. I don't warn people when they buy it that, like any good newspaper, it contains a few lies. And I've grown accustomed, when I feel the tug of a perplexed child on my sleeve, to turn and patiently say: "No, it's not really that big."

Maybe it's comforting to us because we, too, have our blind spots. We, too, have things on the periphery of our lives that we distort — in order to best focus on the things in front of us. In order to best navigate through our days.

Sometimes, though, these things on the periphery, these things that we do not understand, these *far away* things grow to massive proportions — threatening to dwarf our tiny, ordered, known world. And when they get big enough, we are forced to see them for what they are.

People I know are dying.

This is my Greenland Problem. *(It is now dark outside. Someone tries to open the front door and discovers it is locked. Another try. Then, knocking. A pause. Then, more knocking, pounding. And still more. Jody stands in the room, motionless. Knocking and pounding continues. Finally, silence. Jody takes a deep breath. Closes his eyes. He moves to a switch and turns off the lights in the room. He sits. Silence. Phone rings. Jody keeps his eyes closed. Phone keeps ringing. Finally, Jody relents. He goes to the phone and answers it.)*

Jody's Maps. *(Silence. Jody brings the phone away from his head and stares at it. Then he hangs it up and walks to the front*

*door. He opens the door. Carl stands in the doorway, holding a
cordless phone to his ear. Next to him is a chair he has brought.)*
What is it, Carl?

CARL. Do you know what time it is, Jody?

JODY. It's seven forty-five.

CARL. Are you closing early?

JODY. Am I — no, I'm — Carl, what do you —

CARL. It's Friday night.

JODY. I know that.

CARL. You're open till nine on Fridays.

JODY. I know that, Carl.

CARL. The sign says "Closed." The door is locked. The
lights are off. *(Jody abruptly turns the sign around, and turns on
the lights in the room.)*

JODY. There. *(Carl hands Jody his daily mail. Jody grabs it from
him, goes to the cash register, opens it, and looks for a way to stay
busy. Carl brings the chair into the room, takes off his coat, looks
around.)*

CARL. Did you have a good day?

JODY. Mm hmm.

CARL. People are buying maps. That's good. They're still
interested in things. What's water and what's land. Things
like that. *(Silence. Jody keeps busy at the register. Carl walks up
and stares at the Mercator map.)* Hey, Jody. I have a question.

JODY. No. It's not really that big. *(Silence.)*

CARL. It looks bigger than South America.

JODY. It's not.

CARL. Too bad. Think if it was. Think of all the coffee
they could produce. *(Jody just stares at him. Carl grabs a travel
map from a display case. He sits in the most recent chair, peruses
his map. Silence. Finally, Jody relents and talks to him.)*

JODY. And how about you?

CARL. Me?

JODY. How was your day?

CARL. I don't want to disturb you, Jody. You do your work.
I'm contemplating Chad.

JODY. You're not disturbing me. I'm just finishing up. How
was your day?

CARL.   Really?

JODY.   Yes. *(Silence.)*

CARL.   Well, things at the paper are crazy.

JODY.   *(After a moment.)* Really?

CARL.   Yes. Just *crazy*. No one understands, Jody. They really don't. There are all these so-called "reputable" journalists who walk around bitching and moaning how hard it is to cover the news. How *taxing* it is to look around and put into inverted pyramid form something that happened. I should be so lucky, Jody. Do you think I can get away with just typing up stuff that happened? Please. When you write for a tabloid, you have to *create* the news. And believe me, *that* is taxing.

Many's the day I wished I could walk out my door, see a little fire across the street, go to work and type it up: "A little fire happened yesterday across the street." How sweet, how simple. But that little fire is not a story at my paper unless an elderly woman with a foreign accent was washing dishes, and she looks down at the white plate she is scrubbing, and there, there on the white plate she is holding is the face of Jesus, Jesus himself, all beatific and covered with suds — and the face of Jesus speaks to her. The face of Jesus says: "Drop. The. Plate." And the woman is frozen with fear. And again, Jesus says: "Drop. The. Plate." And the woman speaks. The woman says: "It's part of a *set*." Jesus stands firm. "If you want to be with me in heaven, you will drop. The. Plate." The woman is shaking with fear. She tries to explain that it was a wedding gift some forty years ago from an uncle who suffered from polio and died a pauper — but Jesus doesn't give an inch. It's as though he's gone back and read the Old Testament. "I'll give you one more chance," he says, "then I'll have the fire of hell consume your soul." The woman, tears streaming down her face, tries to quickly submerge him under the soapy water — but the water is gone. The sink is gone. Only the plate, and the face, remain. She stares at him, trembling. He says: "Well?" She has a realization. This is not Jesus. This is not her Lord and Savior. This is an *impostor*. This is the spirit of Satan entering the world through her dishware. She looks the plate squarely in the face and says: "I renounce you."

Within seconds, she's toast. So is the building.

The firemen do not find the slightest trace of her. But there, in the midst of the smoking rubble, the dinner plate shines white and pristine. And burned into it forever is the image of the woman's final, hideous expression. The last face she made before she became a china pattern.

My paper can run a story like that. *(Jody stares in disbelief. Carl returns to his travel map.)*

JODY.   Carl?

CARL.   Yes?

JODY.   How do you figure this story gets to the reporter?

CARL.   What do you mean?

JODY.   I mean, she was alone in the room, and now she's dead. So, who witnessed this? Who reported it?

CARL.   Her goldfish.

JODY.   Her —

CARL.   Jody, make an *effort*. Her goldfish survived the fire and channeled the woman's voice into my tape recorder.

JODY.   I see.

CARL.   News is hard, Jody. *(Closes his map.)* So, what's the verdict?

JODY.   Hmm?

CARL.   How'd you do today? Make any money?

JODY.   Well, I wouldn't say it was —

CARL.   There was no money in the drawer, Jody. I saw that.

JODY.   It was slow.

CARL.   Did you close up again?

JODY.   Carl, this is none of your —

CARL.   I'm just asking. I'm just wondering if you *forgot* to keep the shop open. If you forgot to sell things to people today. This is your livelihood, Jody. This is what pays off your plastic.

JODY.   I was out today. I took some time off. I went out.

CARL.   Where?

JODY.   *Where?*

CARL.   Yes, where?

JODY.   Where, like there are places I shouldn't have gone?

Where, like I need your okay before I go?

CARL. Name one place. Name one thing you did.

JODY. No.

CARL. Fine.

JODY. Carl —

CARL. No. That's fine. Let's change the subject. Let's talk about Chad.

JODY. I don't have to tell you where I go, Carl. And I don't have to make things up about my day like you do.

CARL. I don't make things up.

JODY. You don't.

CARL. No. I lie.

JODY. There's a difference?

CARL. There certainly is.

JODY. Do tell.

CARL. If I made it up, that would imply that I wished I was doing it. That I wished I wrote for a tabloid, or restored art or worked at the auto glass shop, or all the rest of it. But I don't wish to do those things.

JODY. Then why do you tell me you do?

CARL. You have to get out, Jody. You weren't out today. I know. Because *I* was out. I was out there driving a rented truck around this neighborhood, packing things, opening and closing doors, going in and out, Jody.

JODY. That's enough. Let's just —

CARL. I was in people's homes today, Jody. I was walking through rooms. This is our *neighborhood*, Jody. You can't hide from it. You can't just —

JODY. Carl —

CARL. You can't just *deny* it.

JODY. I'm going home, Carl. It's been a long day. I'll see you tomorrow. (*Carl does not move.*) You can go ahead. I've got to close up.

CARL. I'll wait.

JODY. You don't have to.

CARL. I'll wait.

JODY. *I'll talk to you tomorrow, Carl. (Carl goes to the door and throws it open.)*

CARL.   I'm waiting for you to leave. I want to watch you walk out this door.

JODY.   For god's sake — *(Jody is putting his mail and a few other items in a small shoulder bag.)*

CARL.   I want to see you go home.

JODY.   Don't push this, Carl. I'm warning you.

CARL.   You certainly are. You've been warning me for some time, but I've been slow to see it. Ordering in food. The sofa in the back room. Seldom a change of clothes. You've been warning me all right. *(Jody grabs his coat, and his shoulder bag. He moves toward the door, then stops, staring at Carl.)*

JODY.   You're in my way. *(Carl backs away from the door and stares at Jody.)*

CARL.   Go ahead. *(Pause.)* There's nothing in your way. *(Longer pause.)* Why don't you go?

JODY.   I want you to leave, Carl. *(Silence. Standoff. Then, Carl leaves. Jody stares at the open door for a moment, then moves to the water cooler. He begins to fill a cup with water, as — Carl bursts back through the door, carrying several chairs. Jody, startled, drops the cup of water.)*

CARL.   *(Moving, talking in a flurry.)* This is fine, Jody. If you won't go out, I'll bring things to you. I'll let you see what you're missing — *(And Carl is out the door again. Jody stares at the chairs. He starts after Carl, but stops.)*

JODY.   Carl. CARL. I DON'T WANT ANY MORE OF YOUR CHAIRS. *(Pause.)* DO YOU HEAR ME? *(Carl is back in — hauling several more chairs, including a wooden rocking chair, with effort.)*

CARL.   No, I don't hear you. I don't hear you at all —

JODY.   *(Overlapping.)* Carl —

CARL.   What are you saying, Jody? I can't understand a word you're saying — *(He sets one of the chairs at Jody's feet — and is gone.)*

JODY.   GODDAMNIT, Carl — *(Jody picks up one of the chairs, in frustration — as though he were about to hurl it across the room — phone rings. Jody is frozen. He drops the chair. He looks at the ringing phone. He moves to the door and begins to slam it shut, but — Carl arrives before he gets the door fully shut. Carl is dragging*

26

eight or ten chairs that have been lashed together with rope. He hauls them to the center of the room.)

CARL.   Phone's ringing, Jody. Someone wants to talk to you —

JODY.   *(Overlapping.)* Enough, Carl. Enough of this game of yours. I don't care if you —

CARL.   What game is that, Jody? I'm playing no *game* here. I went out and got these things — *(And Carl is gone. Jody calls after him, stumbling over chairs on his way to the door.)*

JODY.   I'M LOCKING THIS DOOR, CARL. I DON'T WANT YOU HERE. DO YOU UNDERSTAND ME? I DON'T WANT YOU HERE. *(The phone is still ringing. Jody slams the door shut and locks it. Then, he stumbles over the pile of chairs toward the phone, and answers it.)* Jody's Maps. *(Pause.)* Who? *(A pane of glass in the door is smashed with a chair leg.)* NO, CARL IS NOT HERE. *(Jody slams down the phone, as Carl reaches through the shattered glass and unlocks the door. He throws open the door and brings in another chair.)*

CARL.   That's about it for today, Jody. I'm sure there'll be more in a few days. Who was on the phone?

JODY.   Get out of here.

CARL.   Bobby's dead, Jody.

JODY.   I don't give a *fuck* that Bobby's dead. Do you hear me, Carl? I don't give a fuck.

CARL.   And José. And Michael. And Doug. And Anita —

JODY.   *(Overlapping.)* I know this —

CARL.   And Vince and Jackie and Richard and —

JODY.   I know this, Carl.

CARL.   Do you? I've buried thirty people in six months, Jody. It's gotten to the point where I go to the memorial services to see who's still *alive*.

JODY.   I said I KNOW THIS.

CARL.   I don't think you do. I don't think you see any of it, anymore.

JODY.   What do you want me to do? You want me to march up and down the street shouting MY FRIENDS ARE DYING AND LOOK HOW MUCH I CARE? That does *nothing*, Carl. Do you hear me? *Nothing.*

27

CARL. Jody, you don't —

JODY. THAT BRINGS *NO ONE* BACK. THAT CHANGES *NOTHING.*

CARL. It would change you.

JODY. *Carl?*

CARL. *What?*

JODY. Make someone else your mission. *(Jody slams the door shut. Long silence.)*

CARL. *(Softer.)* Do you recognize these chairs?

JODY. Some of them. *(Silence.)* Not that rocker. *(Silence.)*

CARL. Phillip. *(Silence.)*

JODY. Phillip Carter?

CARL. Phillip Taylor. *(Silence. He touches the back of the last chair he brought in.)* This was Phillip Carter's. *(Silence. Carl sits in the chair and stares front as he speaks.)* I volunteer. I go help move these people — these people's things — out of their homes. And I can't stand the chairs. I can't stand all the empty chairs. Sitting alone in rooms. On the sidewalk outside. Or in the middle of a trimmed green lawn, waiting to be auctioned off to the highest bidder. All these chairs, draped with empty clothes.

JODY. *(Soft.)* What does this *do,* Carl? Does it do something?

CARL. It does for me. This is the thing, Jody: I'm just trying to value my life enough to not throw it into traffic. In the midst of this fucking disease, I'm just trying to find the *worth* of me. And I've stopped trying to find it in grand acts, in major accomplishments. I'm looking for it now in every dish I wash. I'm looking for worth in the way I greet the mailman, the way I make a pot of tea, a letter I actually *write* instead of just *intend.*

Because I don't get much done, Jody. I really don't. I know people who get things done with their days. I admire and despise them. They put their heads on pillows at night and something in their life is actually *different* than it was when they woke up. Those people are mutants to me.

Me — I plan, I plod and I fall short. And if I shorten my plans, I fall still shorter. And if I widen my scope, if I take the long view of *the thing we are living in,* the enormity of it devours me. I see headlines that haunt and silence me. I hear people talk about some Famous Man or Unsuspecting Woman or Innocent Child who got sick — and *yes,* that is *tragic* ...

... But this culture can't just *grieve that life* — they have to place it *above* the others. They have to remind us that *these* people did not deserve it. They didn't do anything *wrong.* They're just normal people. Unlike those *deviants* who got what they *deserved* — these people's death is *wrong.* This Neanderthal Puritanism *chokes at me.* It clouds my perspective and it robs me of my irony. And I need my irony. These days it is standard equipment. It is the penicillin of modern thought. Without my irony, I am just bones that talk. I am just a marksman looking for a bell tower. *(Silence. Softer, now.)*

This is who I am now, Jody. These are my three a.m. thoughts. These are the things that make me spend all morning making the bed not just well, but *perfectly. (Long silence. Finally, Jody moves to the chair he dropped to the ground. He looks down at it. Lifts it. Holds it. Then, stands it upright in the room. After a moment, he walks slowly to the front door. He opens the door. He peers out. Carl turns and watches him. Jody stands motionless, looking out the door for a long time. Finally, he turns back to Carl.)*

JODY.   *(Standing in the doorway.)* I am a boxer. Well, not really a boxer. What happened is that I'd always liked those shorts, those Everlast shorts, and I saw a pair at a thrift store and I bought them. And one day I'm wearing them, and suddenly a cheering crowd of people is all around me, and they are walking me to this ring. This brightly lit ring.

CARL.   In Las Vegas?

JODY.   The dream didn't tell me. It didn't tell me where it was.

CARL.   I love Las Vegas.

JODY.   And I try to tell them that they have the wrong man, that I'm not really a boxer at all, I just happened to buy these shorts at — but they don't listen. I am their champion.

29

I'm sitting on a stool in the corner, and an old man is rubbing my shoulders and talking in my ear, and other people are putting mouthpieces in me and oil on my face. And I feel so ... confident. I can't quite see my opponent across the ring, but I feel so sure, so cocky. The old man is telling me about my jabs, my footwork, my use of the ring. He's telling me about all of it and I am ready.

A bell rings.

I stand up and step forward.

And this is the thing: they will train you, they will teach you to hit, they will teach you to move — but they never tell you about the fear. Nothing the people in your corner can tell you will prepare you for the fear.

There is a huge man in that ring and he plans to omit you. *(Silence.)*

I look back to my corner and — *(Stops.)*

CARL. What? What happens?

JODY. I just remembered something.

CARL. What?

JODY. You are there.

CARL. I am?

JODY. Yes.

CARL. What do I do?

JODY. I ask you for water. I say: "Carl, please, I need some water."

CARL. And I give you some.

JODY. No.

CARL. Sorry.

JODY. You just shove me back into the center of the ring. I tell you I don't want to go, I try to leave the ring to get some water — but you have shoved me back into the center. I can feel my opponent's breath on my face as he circles me. And my arms are so heavy, I'm trying to lift them but they are solid lead, they are hanging at my sides, just *hanging there* — and I'm trying to lift them, lift them in front of my face, I'm trying to lift them to protect myself — *(Jody stops. He turns and looks outside the door. After a moment, he closes the door. He walks into the room and sits in a chair. He stares front. Silence.*

Carl stares at him, then looks over at the water cooler. Carl goes to the water cooler and fills a small cup with water. He brings the water to Jody. Jody takes the cup, without looking at Carl. Simply.) The phone was for you, Carl.

CARL. Thank you.

JODY. Someone has more chairs. *(Silence.)*

CARL. I'll stop by tomorrow. *(Carl goes to the door. He turns the sign from "Open" to "Closed." He leaves, closing the door behind him. He reaches through the broken pane and locks the bolt from the inside. Then, he is gone. Jody stares front. He lifts the cup of water to his mouth and drinks. Lights fade to black.)*

END OF ACT ONE

31

ACT TWO

Scene 1

The room is cluttered with chairs. Everywhere. In some places they are stacked to the ceiling. A few, small pathways provide access to the front door, the water cooler, the cash register. The broken window pane has been boarded up. Morning. The store is "Closed." Jody sits in a large, old-time barber chair. A towel covers his neck and shoulders. He is half-reading a book. Carl stands behind Jody, giving him a haircut.

JODY.   Umm —

CARL.   It — it — it —

JODY.   It was umm — umm —

CARL.   It — it — it —

JODY.   I'll never forget it — it was umm —

CARL.   *(Pointing to the tip of his tongue as he speaks.)* It's here — it's right here — I can almost taste it —

JODY.   It was — umm — oh, for heaven's sake — it was —

CARL.   Umm —

JODY.   You remember, Carl — we all read it —

CARL.   Mm hmm —

JODY.   We sat up late, all of us, night after night, talking about it —

CARL.   Mm hmm —

JODY.   Arguing, debating its pros and cons —

CARL.   Mm hmm —

JODY.   Each and every one of us read it — but I can't —

CARL.   I can't either —

JODY.   Was it —?

CARL.   Hmm?

JODY.   No.

CARL.   Well —

JODY.   Umm —

CARL. I can see the cover —

JODY. I can, too —

CARL. I am reading the cover —

JODY. I'm with you, Carl —

CARL. And the cover says —

JODY. It — it — it —

CARL. It's says, umm —

JODY. It's — it's — it's —

CARL. Gone.

JODY. Damnit.

CARL. Sorry, Jody.

JODY. *It was the book that changed our lives.*

CARL. Right.

JODY. But what was the *name* of it? *(Silence. Carl stops cutting Jody's hair. They both think.)*

CARL. Oh, well. *(Carl resumes cutting.)*

JODY. We remember the wrong things. We remember the combination to our high school gym locker, we forget the name of the woman who taught us to swim. We remember the capitals of states and forget our parent's birthdays. Our friend's middle names. I can recite the periodic table of the elements, but I don't remember the name of the cafe I was sitting in when I realized I'd fallen in love. *(Pause.)* Isn't that odd, Carl?

CARL. What kind of cafe was it? I can check the yellow pages —

JODY. No. I'm sure it's long gone. I just mean, shouldn't we remember those things?

CARL. Like the book that changed our lives?

JODY. Exactly.

CARL. It'll come to you, Jody. Be patient. *(Silence. The haircut continues.)* What are you reading now?

JODY. Ionesco. *The Chairs.* Do you know it?

CARL. Is that the one with the hippos in it?

JODY. No. An old man and woman fill a room with chairs, in expectation of an Orator who they trust will "bequeath their message to the world," who will "radiate upon posterity the light of their minds."

33

CARL. Tall order. What happens?

JODY. Well, once the Orator arrives, the old man and woman throw themselves out the window and fall to their deaths.

CARL. That's tragic.

JODY. Yes.

CARL. But, at least they *get out,* Jody.

JODY. Don't start, Carl.

CARL. So, then what? What does the Orator say?

JODY. He mumbles incoherently. He says nothing.

CARL. And then?

JODY. It's over. *(Long silence. Jody closes the book. Carl clips hair.)*

CARL. Jody?

JODY. Hmm?

CARL. What happens to the chairs?

JODY. Carl, that's not the point.

CARL. Do you know, though? Do you know what happens to all of them?

JODY. *(After a moment.)* No. I don't.

CARL. Maybe the Orator moves in and takes care of them. Maybe he turns the place into a museum and people come and —

JODY. *(Firm.)* Carl. That is not what happens.

CARL. You don't know.

JODY. Yes, I do. It *ends.* That's what happens. It ends.

CARL. But those chairs *belong to someone.* Someone has to deal with them afterwards.

JODY. There is no afterwards. Nothing happens afterwards because it is over. It has ended.

CARL. But the Orator is STILL THERE. He didn't LEAVE. He didn't JUMP OUT THE WINDOW. HE'S STILL THERE. HE HAS NOT ENDED.

JODY. It's a STORY, Carl.

CARL. *(Pause.)* I knew you'd say that. It's a story. It's not real. That's always how these arguments end. Ultimately, everyone falls back on fiction. *(Jody offers the book to Carl.)*

JODY. Here, Carl. Read it yourself. Maybe that will help.

(Carl takes the book. He hands Jody a hand-mirror.)

CARL. Okay. You're done. You're ready for a night on the town. *(Jody checks out his haircut in the mirror as Carl removes the towel and puts the scissors away.)*

JODY. It's —

CARL. What?

JODY. Well, it's —

CARL. What?

JODY. It's *subtle*, Carl.

CARL. You know me.

JODY. *(Looks in mirror, pause.)* Thank you. *(Silence. Jody continues to examine his hair in the mirror.)*

CARL. *What?*

JODY. I usually go down to Water Street. I usually have it cut down there. I'm just used to how they — *(Carl grabs the mirror away from Jody.)*

CARL. Go, then. *(Silence. Carl heads for the door.)* I'm turning the sign, Jody.

JODY. I'm not ready, Carl.

CARL. It's ten-thirty. You should be open.

JODY. It's a mess in here. I need to straighten. There's clutter. There's more than clutter. There's *bulk*.

CARL. All I want to do is turn the sign. It doesn't mean someone will come. Perhaps, today, there is not one person who needs a map.

JODY. Someone does, Carl. I'm certain.

CARL. Perhaps not today. I just want to turn the sign.

JODY. And if someone comes in, what then?

CARL. You'll say hello. You'll answer a question. You'll send them home with Scotland or Chad.

JODY. I don't know, Carl —

CARL. If it goes badly, if it's too hard, you can, well —

JODY. What? I can what?

CARL. You can throw yourself out the window.

JODY. There are chairs in the way.

CARL. I think you'll be fine. *(Carl goes to the sign, takes hold of it, turns back to Jody.)* Jody? *(Jody nods, reluctantly. Carl turns the sign to announce the store is "Open.")* There. *(Jody stands and goes to the cash register for a toothpick to gnaw on. Carl gets a small broom and dust pan — or an electric "dustbuster" — from behind the counter.)*

JODY. Don't you have to work today, Carl?

CARL. I called the shop. They don't need me till later.

JODY. The shop?

CARL. The auto glass shop.

JODY. Oh.

CARL. It was a quiet night for thuggery. There is not much glass to be replaced. *(Carl is finished sweeping up the hair in a matter of seconds.)* There we go.

JODY. Not much hair, Carl.

CARL. I was selective. *(Phone rings.)* Tell them I'm on my way. *(Carl gets his coat as Jody answers the phone.)*

JODY. *(Into phone.)* He's on his way. Yes. Goodbye. *(Carl starts for the door. Jody hangs up the phone.)* Carl —

CARL. I've got to go. *(Carl starts out the door.)*

JODY. What else have I forgotten, Carl?

CARL. *(Stops.)* What?

JODY. I've forgotten the name of that book that changed our lives. I've forgotten the name of that cafe. What *else* have I forgotten? What else do I think I know that I really *don't*?

CARL. *(Quickly.)* Ed's Cafe. Rita's Cafe. Old Timer's Cafe. Half Moon Cafe. Joe and Bob's Cafe —

JODY. No, Carl. Forget the cafe.

CARL. I never knew it. You're the one that —

JODY. We don't know our minds, Carl. We don't get a printout. Nothing in our minds warns us it's going. It just goes. And something else follows. And our last thought is left to turn out the lights.

CARL. LOOK, if you don't like your haircut, just SAY IT.

JODY. Close the door, Carl.

CARL. They're waiting for —

JODY. Please. *(Silence. Carl closes the door.)* You've been a good friend to me, Carl. Even when I've wanted to kill you. You're like the little brother I never wanted to have.

CARL. Thank you.

JODY. But, I don't *know you*, Carl. I don't really know you.

When you go home to your apartment at night, and you close the door behind you — I have no idea what you do. *(Pause.)* What chair you sit in. What song you hum. *(Pause.)* I think about that a lot, Carl.

CARL.   *(After a moment.)* Well, the chair part is easy. I only have one chair. It's a classic 1950s kitchen chair, silver with a bright turquoise seat.

JODY.   That was a figure of speech, Carl —

CARL.   You've seen it, haven't you, Jody? You've seen my turquoise kitchen chair?

JODY.   Yes.

CARL.   It's a collector's item. The turquoise seat is actually —

JODY.   Carl.

CARL.   What?

JODY.   We don't know people.

CARL.   It's a mystery, Jody. Like people who knowingly buy jackets with fringe on them. It's an absolute mystery.

JODY.   I'm talking about our friends. Who are really our friends? We don't know.

CARL.   Do this: Pack up and move on two days notice. See who helps you. *Those* are your friends.

JODY.   You're missing the —

CARL.   I answered this ad. It said: Are you interested in a cruelty-free relationship? (Well, I think, there's a first time for everything.) So, I make plans to meet this man at the park. We have agreed upon a time and a bench. Then, we have made plans to have a quiet cup of coffee. I go to the park. I like the park. I like to walk around the lake and look at the babies and dogs. I sit on the bench with my expectations. I am expecting a man who is just plain no-debate handsome. Someone who could pull off one of those black turtleneck *Hamlets*. The man approaches. My expectations are nowhere in sight. He is one of those men who honestly believes he can iron his shirt by tucking it in. And his breath. It was not just bad, it was *ancient*. I'm telling you, Jody, something had crawled down in there and *died*. He didn't need mouthwash, he needed *archaeology*.

JODY.   So, what happened?

CARL. Nothing happened. We didn't even get as far as the coffee. He bored me to tears for ten minutes and I left. I saw him a week later, and he avoided me like I was carrying a clipboard at an airport.

JODY. But, what is your *point?*

CARL. Yesterday that man took his car and mowed down twenty people at a sidewalk cafe. *(Pause.)* A reporter asked him why. *(Pause.)* He said: I just couldn't look at them anymore. *(Silence. Jody stares at him, still waiting for the point.)* Maybe it's better not to know. *(Carl starts for the door.)*

JODY. We trick ourselves. *(Carl stops.)* We add up our time with someone, we arrive at a number of hours or days or years, and we check that number against a chart on the wall. And the chart on the wall says: If you've spent X number of years with so and so, you must know them well. I no longer believe the chart on the wall.

CARL. Give me an example.

JODY. WHAT DO YOU DO FOR A LIVING? There's an example.

CARL. I've told you.

JODY. You've told me many things.

CARL. I do many things. *(Opens door.)* They're waiting for me, Jody —

JODY. You tell lies.

CARL. Yes.

JODY. You create occupations.

CARL. Yes.

JODY. Why?

CARL. For the same reason I create you, Jody. *(Pause.)* So, I have something to hold onto. I don't know what chair *you* sit in, Jody. I don't know what song *you* hum — though, I suspect it's something pretty dated and embarrassing — I don't know much about you, either, except that you love your store and your maps and lately you will not leave, you *will not go out there. (Pause.)* So, I create you. I create the part of you that does stuff while I'm not around. *(Pause.)* That's what people do, Jody. That's the closest they get to knowing each other. *(Silence.)*

JODY. Can we play our game, Carl?

CARL. The game where we tell the truth?

JODY. Yes.

CARL. Sure. *(Jody stands and approaches Carl.)*

JODY. I have to go out, Carl.

CARL. *(Soft.)* I know.

JODY. I have to be tested. *(Silence.)*

CARL. You've been tested. *(Pause.)* Every six months for the past few years.

JODY. No. *(Pause.)* No.

CARL. You've told me you —

JODY. *No. (Silence.)*

CARL. I'll go with you.

JODY. Can you find someone who'll come here? Someone who'll come here and test me here?

CARL. I'll try, Jody. I'll make some calls.

JODY. Thank you. *(Phone rings.)*

CARL. Tell them I've left. Say I've left. *(Carl goes. Jody answers the phone.)*

JODY. *(Into phone.)* Jody's Maps. *(Pause.)* Yes. He left. He'll be right there. *(Jody hangs up the phone. He looks around his shop. He points to a spot on a large map or standing globe. He turns to the audience.)* When I was a teenager, I pumped gas in the middle of Montana. A little station alone in the Big Sky Country. Sign out front: "Next Gas, Two Hundred Miles." That's where I learned my geography. Folks'd pull up and say "How far is it to such and such? Can I make such and such by nightfall? And what about so and so — is that straight north of here?" At the end of every day I tried in vain to wash the diesel off my hands. And then I'd sit down with my father's atlas, open it up … and see how many lies I'd told people that day. *(Music begins softly: Intro and first verse of a song such as Bob Dylan's "I Shall Be Released,"* sung by Joe Cocker.)* I haven't forgotten that. *(Music builds.)*

---

* See Special Note on Songs and Recordings on copyright page.

Scene 2

More chairs. Evening. The store is "Closed."

Jody sits in a chair, sewing a button onto a shirt. As he sews, he hums a song such as the Joe Cocker version of Bob Dylan's "I Shall Be Released."*

After a moment, a key opens the front door and Carl enters. Carl carries three chairs, a sack of food from the deli, and a small plastic bag.

CARL.   Ask me where I've been. Go on, just ask me.

JODY.   Where've you been, Carl?

CARL.   I've been out not smoking, not drinking and not getting laid. I've been out there watching my step and not doing anything, *anything* in the least bit reckless or spontaneous. I've been out there acting like I'm not out there. *God,* life is grand.

JODY.   What's to eat?

CARL.   Not dessert. Not sugar. Not caffeine. Not cholesterol. *(opens the sack, lifts food out.)* It's ... BLAND SOUP AND BREAD.

JODY.   Again?

CARL.   Yes, again. *(Carl removes a second container of soup from the sack, as well as two plastic spoons.)*

JODY.   Makes me want to pour whiskey on a steak and smoke it.

CARL.   Now, now, Jody. At this point in the century, we know better. We are no longer hunter-gatherers. We are browser-nibblers.

JODY.   Did you get butter?

---

* See Special Note on Songs and Recordings on copyright page.

CARL. *Please,* Jody. *(Carl removes three large white candles from the plastic bag, sets them on a surface and lights them, during the following.)* You know what happened just before the dinosaurs went extinct?

JODY. No, Carl.

CARL. They changed diets. Think about it.

JODY. Is that true?

CARL. It's what I tell my students at the University. *(Jody stares at him. They settle down into two of the newest chairs and begin eating.)*

JODY. You asked them, Carl? You did?

CARL. I told you I did.

JODY. I want to be sure.

CARL. I spent all week on the phone with them. They don't make exceptions. I tried, Jody. But, they won't come here and give you your test. You have to go there.

JODY. And the other places?

CARL. I called all of them. *(Stands.)* Here. I'll get the phone book. You can call them yourself.

JODY. Sit down, Carl. I believe you.

CARL. It's five blocks, Jody. It's a lovely walk. You'll like it. *(Jody stares at him.)* Okay. You'll hate it. Maybe you'll get hit by a car. Would that cheer you up?

JODY. Eat your soup. *(Carl sits and resumes eating.)*

CARL. They're good people. I've been there twice.

JODY. When were you there last?

CARL. About six months ago.

JODY. You're due to go again, aren't you?

CARL. As a precaution, yes.

JODY. Come with me.

CARL. No.

JODY. But you have to go, anyway.

CARL. I'm going next week. You're going on your own. Deal with it. *(Pause.)* They close at eight tonight.

JODY. I know.

CARL. I know you know. *(Carl stares at him.)*

JODY. I'm GOING, Carl. I'm GOING TONIGHT. Are you happy?

CARL. I'm happy, take my picture. *(Silence.)*

JODY. Did you work today?

CARL. I can't talk about it.

JODY. Why?

CARL. It's scandalous.

JODY. The tabloid?

CARL. No. The glass shop.

JODY. *(After a moment.)* What can be scandalous about an auto-glass shop? *(Silence.)*

CARL. Well. Okay. But, what I'm about to say can't leave this room.

JODY. Don't worry.

CARL. *(Pause.)* The man who runs the shop — I'll call him Mr. "R" — has been having some tough financial times. So ... Mr. "R" enlists the help of his delinquent son — whom I'll call "Tad." "Tad," it seems, has been very, very bad. So ... father and son strike a deal. Mr. "R" will refrain from sending "Tad" to a military academy, if "Tad" and his little delinquent friends will do Mr. "R" a favor. So, last night, "Tad" was bad. He and his little friends take a 3 a.m. joyride through several neighborhoods, smashing every car window they find. Before calling it a night, they sever the phone cables of the competing auto glass stores.

The next day, Mr. "R's" business has grown twenty-fold.

JODY. How can they get away with that?

CARL. Mr. "H."

JODY. Who?

CARL. The chief of police.

JODY. You're kidding.

CARL. You didn't hear it from me.

JODY. That's amazing, Carl.

CARL. I'm telling you, Jody, there's some heavy hitters working down at that shop. Guys with connections that'd curl your toes.

JODY. You sure can pick 'em.

CARL. There's a man installs windshields down there who used to be a *municipal worker* in Dallas.

JODY. So?

CARL. Jody, this guy *mowed the Grassy Knoll.* *(Pause.)* That's all I can say about it. *(Carl gathers up his empty food containers and throws them away. He watches Jody. Jody continues sewing the button on his shirt. He hums, as before.)* It's seven-thirty.

JODY. I know that.

CARL. You want help with your shirt?

JODY. No.

CARL. They close at eight.

JODY. I *know that,* Carl. *(Silence. Jody sews. Carl gathers up Jody's food container and throws it away.)* If I don't make it, I'll go tomorrow.

CARL. They're closed tomorrow.

JODY. Monday, then. *(Silence. Carl stares at him. Jody sews. Carl blows out the candles — and, after doing so, his eyes land on a large map on one of the walls. He stares at the map.)*

CARL. Weird. *(Pause.)* Weird.

JODY. What's that?

CARL. This map. *(Pause.)* Weird.

JODY. You've seen that before.

CARL. Not really. I never really noticed.

JODY. That's the Peter's Projection map. It's an equal area map.

CARL. A what?

JODY. It lets you accurately compare the sizes of all the countries.

CARL. But, the shapes are weird.

JODY. That's because the projection is —

CARL. It's like Salvador Dali took some continents and melted them.

JODY. They're as accurate as the shapes on the Mercator map. You're just used to the other.

CARL. So, these are the real sizes?

JODY. Yes.

CARL. So, Chad is bigger than the entire American west coast?

JODY. Yes, it is.

CARL. Go, Chad.

JODY. And the equator is in the center of the map, instead

43

of relegating the southern hemisphere to the bottom third.

CARL. I don't know, Jody.

JODY. What?

CARL. The people in Greenland must be pissed.

JODY. This map solves the Greenland problem. I envy them that.

CARL. Yeah. But, everything looks weird.

JODY. It's a trade-off, Carl. It bends your preconceptions to achieve accuracy.

CARL. *(Directly to Jody.)* It tells us what we need to know.

JODY. Exactly. *(Silence. Then, Jody resumes sewing.)*

CARL. Jody?

JODY. Hmm?

CARL. You've been done sewing that button for a while. You can stop now. *(Jody looks at Carl. Then, he stops sewing. He bites the end of the thread. He holds the shirt, tightly. Carl moves very close to Jody. He looks at him. Silence. Carl reaches into his pocket and slowly pulls out a Mounds candy bar. He smiles.)*

JODY. *(Smiles.)* Guilty pleasures.

CARL. The only kind worth having. *(Carl sits near Jody. Gives him half the Mounds bar, keeps the other half for himself.)* Cheers. *(They "toast" and then delicately bite into their candy. It is naughty and delicious. They moan with delight.)*

JODY. Oh.

CARL. Mm hmm.

JODY. It is so … *(With delight.)* bad for us.

CARL. That's today's view. Tomorrow's research may reveal the opposite. Someday this may be part of a healthy, balanced diet.

JODY. God, I hope not. *(Takes a bite, savors it.)* I like it just the way it is. *(They eat.)*

CARL. I know you're scared, Jody. *(Silence.)* The not knowing is worse. Being left alone with your imagination is worse. *(Silence.)*

JODY. Nobody can just be "sick," anymore. Sometimes I can barely remember that "sick" used to mean you had a cold, or the flu. Now, you ask how someone is. You're told they're "sick." And you know exactly what that means. *(Long silence.)*

Look at this place, Carl.

CARL. *(Soft.)* I know.

JODY. It's obscene. And every minute you're hauling chairs in here, there are people out there making the world a safer place to live. They are out there fighting *language* that is obscene, *pictures* that are obscene, *movies* that are obscene. We should be so lucky. Imagine if our safety depended on protecting our children from *words*, from *ideas*, from *pictures of people's bodies*. Imagine if those things were our great plague. *(Pause.)* We should be so fucking lucky. *(Silence. Jody stands and puts the shirt on. After a moment, he stares at the front door, then stands, motionless. Carl fills the silence.)*

CARL. Hey, Jody.

JODY. Hmm?

CARL. What was that song?

JODY. Which?

CARL. The one you've been humming.

JODY. *(Pause, smiles a bit.)* Mr. Dylan's "I Shall Be Released," as interpreted by Mr. Joe Cocker.* *(Pause.)* Everyone has one song that can never be turned up too loud. That's mine.

CARL. I never knew that. *(Jody gets his shoulder bag and coat.)* I guess I expected something more —

JODY. What?

CARL. I don't know. Something more … Sinatra-ey.

JODY. Carl. *Please.* *(Jody puts on his jacket, then stands, staring at the door. After a moment, Carl again fills the silence.)*

CARL. Hey, Jody?

JODY. Hmm?

CARL. Do you have a copy of it here?

JODY. No.

CARL. Not anywhere?

JODY. It's at home. *(Jody opens the door. He stands in the doorway, staring out, motionless. Again, after a long moment, Carl*

---

* If it is necesssary to use a different song, this sentence should
  be changed to read: … "(Name of Song) by (Name of Singer)."

45

speaks.)

CARL. Jody?

JODY. *(Gently.)* Carl. You have to shut up, now.

CARL. I was going to get you some water. You want some? *(Jody looks at Carl, then nods. Carl gets two cups of water, brings one to Jody. They drink their water.)* I'll keep an eye on things, here. *(Pause.)* I've never run a map store before.

JODY. It was just a matter of time. *(They are standing under the huge photo of planet Earth. Jody looks up at it as he sips his water.)*

CARL. It'll be okay, Jody. *(Silence.)*

JODY. The astronauts of Apollo 17 took this photo. It's become the definitive image of our planet. They may have taken it with the intent of showing the grandeur, the enormity of the earth. But, they captured something else, instead. Humility. *(Quietly, reverently.)* From the Latin: *humus.* Meaning: earth. They captured a planet, small and alone, surrounded by enormous darkness. *(Silence. They sip their water.)*

CARL. *(Soft.)* Hey, Jody.

JODY. Hmm?

CARL. You know what's great about us?

JODY. *(Smiles.)* No, Carl. What's great about us?

CARL. We never fell in love. *(Pause.)* All these years, all that's happened. We never did.

JODY. No. We never did. *(Silence.)*

CARL. And I'm glad, you know, because the thing is, the thing about meeting people is this: lovers are easy, *friends* are hard. The right combination of small talk and clothing will land you a lover. Friends, though, are a mystery.

JODY. Jackets with fringe.

CARL. Exactly. *(Silence.)* Why do you think that is, Jody?

JODY. Hmm?

CARL. That we never fell in love.

JODY. You're a nuthead, Carl.

CARL. Yeah, but at least I'm not a map-geek. *(Silence. They smile. They sip water.)* Let's never do. No matter *what.* Okay?

JODY. Okay. *(Silence.)*

CARL. Do you have the address?

JODY. Yes. *(Jody throws away his paper cup, picks up his bag. Stops.)* Wait for me, Carl?

CARL. I'm not going anywhere. And when you're finished, we'll kick up our heels. We'll put on Joe Cocker, get drunk, tell lies and make promises we can't keep. It'll be *great. (Silence. Jody smiles.)*

JODY. I'll see you later, Carl.

CARL. You will. *(Jody leaves the store, closing the door behind him. Carl watches him go. Silence. Then, Carl goes to his coat and gets a stack of envelopes. He also gets some sheets of stamps. He sits in the room and begins to affix stamps to the numerous envelopes. As he does so, he begins talking to the audience. As Carl speaks, the lights in the room gradually shift from evening ... to dawn ... to morning.)*

Here's something I've thought about: Why aren't there stamps for the things you *don't* want to mail?

I have a stack of bills here. I am mailing them to organizations that have been badgering me, threatening me to give them their money or else. I've tried to reason with them, but although their commercials depict them as companies with big hearts — I have found them to have big hearts of *ice.* So, I succumb to their threats and prepare to mail them their blood money.

And now it's time for the stamp. And what kind of stamps do I attach to these things I don't want to mail? Little *flowers. Birds.* Cuddly animals and smiling poets. I attach stamps that say *love,* and *peace,* and *joy.*

This sends the wrong message.

I want stamps that say: HERE'S YOUR FUCKING MONEY, NOW SHUT UP. I want stamps with pictures of raw sewage and Mussolini. I want skull-and-crossbone stamps that have warnings from the Surgeon General. *(He looks at one of the stamps he is about to affix.)*

I've had it with giving flowers to the wrong people. *(He affixes the stamp. Stops. Silence.)*

A life is such a lot of paperwork. I do what I can. I try to keep the stacks of bills and claims and counter-claims from reaching mythic proportions. But, I fall short. *(He holds up the stack of envelopes.)*

None of these people had time to finish their paperwork. Robert was too busy restoring art. The tabloid that Jeremy wrote for refused to pay his health costs. Eric watered the corporations plants but couldn't get a loan from them. Bridget had her tenure denied by the University. And Franklin ... Franklin just threw 'em all away. If it had a picture window, he threw it in the trash with all the other broken windows, then he cranked up his radio and installed another windshield.

They say fame is when a lot of people you've never met celebrate your death. None of these people were famous. Like most the people taken by this disease, we in the general public murdered them twice. First, by romanticizing them. Glamorizing their grief. And, then by ignoring them.

My friend, Hank, worked for the police department. He dusted crime scenes for fingerprints. He loved his job (except for the paperwork, he said). And he was good at it.

When a cop is killed in the line of duty, the entire force turns out for the funeral. Speeches are made. The anger is channeled into ceremony.

When Hank died, there was no one. The "official" line was that since Hank did not die in the line of duty, a ceremony would not be appropriate. I called one of his co-workers and got the "unofficial" line: "If we'd gone, it'd look like we approved of what he *did*." *(He affixes the final stamp.)* The paperwork is all that's left. The unfinished business. *(The front door opens and Jody enters. He wears a fresh change of clothes.)*

JODY. Hello, Carl.

CARL. Hello, stranger.

JODY. You've forgotten the sign. *(Jody turns the sign to read "Open.")* It's nine o'clock, Carl. We're supposed to be open.

CARL. Sorry, Jody. I was catching up on paperwork.

JODY. *(Smiles.)* I hope you didn't forget the sign all week.

CARL. No, I didn't. I didn't sell a lot of maps, though. Fewer people than I thought shared my interest in Chad. And people seemed to think the shop was sort of —

JODY. What?

CARL.   Cluttered. I told them you'd be back today. I told them you'd taken the week off. *(Silence.)* How was it?

JODY.   The test?

CARL.   The week. Out there. *(Silence.)*

JODY.   They drew the blood from my arm. And I left. And I walked home. *(Pause.)* The long way. *(Pause.)* Past everything that was familiar. Past everything that had a memory attached to it. I walked every day like that. And as I walked, I remembered.

CARL.   The name of the book?

JODY.   Not, yet. But I'll get it. I had a week where I believed I could remember everything. *(Pause.)* I'm glad you made me go out, Carl. *(Silence.)*

CARL.   When do you get your results?

JODY.   Today.

CARL.   In person?

JODY.   No. I can call. *(Silence. Then, Carl puts his envelopes in his coat and prepares to leave.)*

CARL.   Well, I'll let you get settled in here. Maybe you'll have better luck than me at selling those weird-shaped maps.

JODY.   They're accurate, Carl. They tell us what we need to know. *(Carl stares at him. Jody walks to the counter and looks at the phone. Carl starts to leave, quietly.)* Carl. *(Carl stops.)* Stay with me. *(Carl tosses his coat on a chair. Jody takes a card out of his wallet, sits behind the counter, and is about to dial a number written on the card. He stops. Silence.)* How 'bout you? How was your week?

CARL.   It was busy. There was a theft at the museum.

JODY.   Did they take the Hopper?

CARL.   The what?

JODY.   The one you restored?

CARL.   I have no idea, Jody. That's not my job. I go in, I dust for fingerprints, I run 'em through the computer. Prints talk, Jody. Prints talk and they never lie.

JODY.   Imagine that. *(Silence. Jody looks at the card in front of him.)*

CARL.   Hey. Did you rem —

JODY.   *(Smiles.)* Archie's. Archie's Cafe. It came to me last night. *(Silence. Jody dials a number written on the card. Carl has a seat. Jody speaks into the phone.)* Yes. I'm calling for my test results. *(Reads a number off the card.)* 1 5 7 2 2 dash 7 6 dash 8 3. *(An extremely long silence, as Jody waits for the results.)* Jody. *(Pause.)* Yes, I'll hold. *(Another still longer silence. Finally ...)* Yes, I'm here. *(Pause, he waits, then says simply.)* Thank you. *(Pause, begins to hang up, stops.)* What? Oh, that was a question I had when I — you can disregard — *(Stops.)* I didn't know that. Thank you. *(He hangs up the phone. Carl stares at him.)* It's negative. *(Silence.)*

CARL. *(Soft.)* It's negative.

JODY. *(Also soft.)* Yes. *(Jody moves away from the counter, slowly. He looks around the room. Carl stands, watching him. Then, Jody moves to Carl. They embrace. As they release each other, Jody says ...)* And you know what else, Carl?

CARL. *(Smiling.)* What?

JODY. If I need another test some day, and I'm unable to leave my home — they'll send someone here.

CARL. They *said* that?

JODY. You knew that, Carl.

CARL. *(Pause.)* Yes. I knew that. *(Jody stands in the middle of the room.)* How does it feel? *(Silence.)*

JODY. I was talking to a man in the waiting room, before I went in. He was paging through a magazine, waiting for a friend who was being tested. This man told me he came to this city in 1980, planning to be wild and live out all the fantasies he'd harbored for so long. But, instead, right away, I met someone and fell in love. They were together for eight years. This man closed his magazine and looked up at me. "Falling in love," he said, "saved my life." *(Phone rings. Carl stares at Jody, then heads for the door.)*

CARL. Tell them I'm on my way. *(Music: "I Shall Be Released"* — verse two.)*

* See Special Note on Songs and Recordings on copyright page.

Scene 3

In a shaft of light we see a 1950s silver kitchen chair, with a turquoise seat. Nothing else.

Jody stands, looking at the chair for a long time. Then, he looks at the audience.

JODY.   One night, a few months later, I saw a chair here. *(Pause.)* I looked at it. I sat in it. *(He sits, pause.)* A chair. Nothing else. *(Lights expand to reveal the store. Night. The store is "Open." The room remains cluttered with chairs. Jody sits in the chair, staring front, for a long time. Phone rings. He looks at the phone, then goes to it. He answers it.)* Yes? *(He looks at the front door. He sets the phone aside, goes quickly to the door, and opens it. Carl, wearing a long black coat, stands in the doorway, holding his cordless phone to his ear.)*

CARL.   Your sign says you're open. Are you open?

JODY.   Yes.

CARL.   Can we talk, Jody?

JODY.   Sure.

CARL.   Can we talk on the phone?

JODY.   On the —?

CARL.   I wanted to call and talk to you on the phone, but I didn't want to be alone, so I came over. *(Silence. Carl gestures to Jody's phone. Jody stares at him, then goes to his phone and picks it up. Standing behind his counter, Jody speaks on his phone.)*

JODY.   How's this?

CARL.   Good. *(Pause.)* It's bright in here, Jody. Can I light these?

JODY.   Sure. *(Carl lights the large white candles, which are just beneath the huge photo of planet Earth. Then, he turns off the lights in the room.)*

CARL.   Good, yes?

JODY.   Yes. *(In silence, Carl walks to the furthest corner of the room away from Jody. He crouches there, amid the stacks of chairs.*

51

From this point till noted at the end, the men speak only into their telephones.) What did you want to talk about, Carl? *(Silence.)* What did you do today? Was there art to be restored, was there —

CARL.   No. All the art's been restored, all the broken glass has been fixed. Things are in order, Jody. *(Silence. The room darkens.)* Did you find my chair, Jody?

JODY.   I did.

CARL.   It's a good chair, don't you think? Sturdy.

JODY.   Yes.

CARL.   A person could sit in it. A person could peruse a map. Plan a trip.

JODY.   It's a good chair, Carl. *(Silence.)*

CARL.   "We will leave some traces, for we are people and not cities."

JODY.   *(Smiles a bit.)* Ionesco. You read it.

CARL.   I liked that line. *(Silence.)* Will you keep my chair, Jody?

JODY.   I will.

CARL.   That would make me happy.

JODY.   Good.

CARL.   *(Soft.)* I'm happy, take my picture. *(Silence. The room darkens.)* Hey, Jody?

JODY.   Yes?

CARL.   Any good dreams? *(Silence.)*

JODY.   *(Not into the phone.)* Carl —

CARL.   *Please,* Jody. *(Silence. The room darkens. Jody lifts the phone to his head and speaks.)*

JODY.   I am ... at a concert. Outdoors. And on the way to this concert, I've stopped at a thrift store and bought a big black turtleneck and a black leather jacket, and thick, black sunglasses.

CARL.   Fringe, Jody?

JODY.   On the jacket?

CARL.   Yes.

JODY.   No, Carl.

CARL.   Good.

JODY.   And I'm standing there, looking up at the moon, waiting for the band to come on — and suddenly a group of people is ushering me backstage. They're introducing me to the rest of my band, there are sound and light guys running around with headphones and cables — and I'm trying to tell them: I think you have the *wrong person*. This is not my band. I'm not a singer. I just bought these clothes at a thrift store and — the next thing I know, I'm at center stage. A spotlight hits me in the eyes. The band launches into the song.

CARL.   What song, Jody?

JODY.   My favorite song, Carl. And my band is looking at me and waiting for me to sing. I close my eyes. I hear the crowd screaming. I hear the music rumbling under me. I open my mouth ... *and I am singing that song, Carl.* I am singing that song like Joe Cocker. I am doing Mr. Dylan proud. And the crowd is — *(Stops.)*

CARL.   What?

JODY.   I just remembered something.

CARL.   What?

JODY.   You are there.

CARL.   I am?

JODY.   Yes, you are. You are standing right next to me, Carl. You've been to the same thrift store.

CARL.   Do I look okay?

JODY.   You look great. And we are *singing*, Carl.

CARL.   I'm singing, too?

JODY.   The band is shaking the rafters behind us, the crowd is shouting and swaying. And we are together, Carl. We are together. And we are singing. *(Long silence. Carl puts his phone inside his coat. He sits, staring front. Jody hangs up his phone, quietly.)*

CARL.   Jody?

JODY.   Hmm?

CARL.   Can I stay here tonight?

JODY.   Of course you can.

CARL.   Thanks. *(Silence. Music: The final verse and chorus of*

53

"I Shall Be Released"* begins, very softly. Jody looks at Carl. Then, he stands, puts on his coat and moves to the door. He turns the sign to read "Closed." He pulls the shade. He turns back to Carl, indicating the lit candles.)

JODY. Carl?

CARL. Hmm?

JODY. Should I —

CARL. Yes. *(Music builds. Jody walks to the candles. He takes a long look at the photo of planet Earth. He blows out the candles. Jody opens the door, looks back at Carl. In the musical break prior to the final phrase of the song, Jody speaks.)*

JODY. I'll see you in the morning, Carl.

CARL. You will. *(Jody leaves, closing the door behind him. As the song ends, lights fade to black on Carl.)*

END OF PLAY

* See Special Note on Songs and Recordings on copyright page.

AUTHOR'S NOTE

The following was written for the original production of the play at Northlight Theatre, Evanston,   Illinois.

LEAVING SOME TRACES

"To hope for better times must not be a feeling,
but an *action* in the present."
— Vincent Van Gogh

My parents taught me that an act of kindness is its own reward. That took awhile to sink in. Over time, I have begun to appreciate the depth of their wisdom. I thought of this recently while doing research for a new play I'm writing about Joyce Cheeka, a young Squaxin Indian girl growing up in the Pacific Northwest in the '20s. One phrase from the teachings of her elders keeps coming up again and again: *be useful.*

In the midst of a world that is too big and too fast, a world where information rules like a dictator and news travels like a virus, it is easy to be overcome by the hopelessness of the world and the helplessness of we, its keepers. What impact can we hope to have? What traces will we leave behind?

History, I believe, is not the story of grand acts and masterpieces. History, instead, is the inexorable accumulation of tiny events — footsteps and glances, hands in soil, broken promises, bursts of laughter, weapons and wounds, hands touching hair, the art of conversation, the rage of loss. Historians may focus on the famous, familiar names — but history itself is made, day after day, by all those whose names are never known, all those who never made a proclamation or held an office, all those who were handed a place on earth and quietly made a life out of it.

So, what do we affect during our lifetime? What, ultimately, is our legacy? I believe, in most cases, our legacy is our friends. We write our history onto them, and they walk with us through our days like time capsules, filled with our mutual past, the fragments of our hearts and minds. Our friends get our uncensored questions and our yet-to-be-reasoned opinions. Our friends grant us the chance to make our grand, embarrassing, contradictory pronouncements about the world. They get the very best, and are stuck with the absolute worst, we have to offer. Our friends get our rough drafts. Over time, they both open our eyes and break our hearts.

Emerson wrote "Make yourself necessary to someone." In a chaotic world, friendship is the most elegant, the most lasting way to be *useful*. We are, each of us, a living testament to our friends' compassion and tolerance, humor and wisdom, patience and grit. Friendship, not technology, is the only thing capable of showing us the enormity of the world.

> "For the world is not to be narrowed till it will go
> into the understanding (which has been done hitherto),
> but the understanding is to be expanded and opened
> till it can take in the image of the world."
> — Francis Bacon

Welcome to Jody's Maps. We're glad you're here.

Steven Dietz
December, 1992
Evanston, Illinois

PROPERTY LIST

Chair (JODY)
Wrapped toothpick (JODY)
Open-Closed sign (JODY)
Paper cups (JODY, CARL)
Long, rolled-up, wrapped maps (JODY, CARL)
Mercator projection world map (JODY)
Cordless telephone (CARL)
Daily mail (CARL)
Travel map (CARL)
Small shoulder bag (JODY)
Coat (JODY)
Several chairs (CARL) including:
  1 wooden rocking chair
  8-10 chairs lashed together with rope
Towel (JODY)
Book (JODY)
Hand mirror (CARL)
Scissors (CARL)
Small broom and dustpan (or Dustbuster) (CARL)
Shirt (JODY)
Button (JODY)
Sewing needle (JODY)
Thread (JODY)
Front door key (CARL)
Sack of food (CARL) including:
  2 containers of soup
  2 plastic spoons
  bread
Small plastic bag (CARL)
3 large white candles (CARL)
Matches or lighter (CARL)
Mounds candy bar (CARL)
Coat (CARL)

Small paper cups
Stack of envelopes (CARL)
Sheet of stamps (CARL)
Wallet (JODY) with:
        business card

SOUND EFFECTS

Telephone rings

NEW PLAYS

★ **HONOUR by Joanna Murray-Smith.** In a series of intense confrontations, a wife, husband, lover and daughter negotiate the forces of passion, history, responsibility and honour. "HONOUR makes for surprisingly interesting viewing. Tight, crackling dialogue (usually played out in punchy verbal duels) captures characters unable to deal with emotions ... Murray-Smith effectively places her characters in situations that strip away pretense." –*Variety* "... the play's virtues are strong: a distinctive theatrical voice, passionate concerns ... HONOUR might just capture a few honors of its own." –*Time Out Magazine* [1M, 3W] ISBN: 0-8222-1683-3

★ **MR. PETERS' CONNECTIONS by Arthur Miller.** Mr. Miller describes the protagonist as existing in a dream-like state when the mind is "freed to roam from real memories to conjectures, from trivialities to tragic insights, from terror of death to glorying in one's being alive." With this memory play, the Tony Award and Pulitzer Prize-winner reaffirms his stature as the world's foremost dramatist. "... a cross between Joycean stream-of-consciousness and Strindberg's dream plays, sweetened with a dose of William Saroyan's philosophical whimsy ... CONNECTIONS is most intriguing ..." –*The NY Times* [5M, 3W] ISBN: 0-8222-1687-6

★ **THE WAITING ROOM by Lisa Loomer.** Three women from different centuries meet in a doctor's waiting room in this dark comedy about the timeless quest for beauty – and its cost. "... THE WAITING ROOM ... is a bold, risky melange of conflicting elements that is ... terrifically moving ... There's no resisting the fierce emotional pull of the play." –*The NY Times* "... one of the high points of this year's Off-Broadway season ... THE WAITING ROOM is well worth a visit." –*Back Stage* [7M, 4W, flexible casting] ISBN: 0-8222-1594-2

★ **THE OLD SETTLER by John Henry Redwood.** A sweet-natured comedy about two church-going sisters in 1943 Harlem and the handsome young man who rents a room in their apartment. "For all of its decent sentiments, THE OLD SETTLER avoids sentimentality. It has the authenticity and lack of pretense of an Early American sampler." –*The NY Times* "We've had some fine plays Off-Broadway this season, and this is one of the best." –*The NY Post* [1M, 3W] ISBN: 0-8-222-1642-6

★ **LAST TRAIN TO NIBROC by Arlene Hutton.** In 1940 two young strangers share a seat on a train bound east only to find their paths will cross again. "All aboard. LAST TRAIN TO NIBROC is a sweetly told little chamber romance." –*Show Business* "... [a] gently charming little play, reminiscent of Thornton Wilder in its look at rustic Americans who are to be treasured for their simplicity and directness ..." –*Associated Press* "The old formula of boy wins girls, boy loses girl, boy wins girl still works ... [a] well-made play that perfectly captures a slice of small-town-life-gone-by." –*Back Stage* [1M, 1W] ISBN: 0-8222-1753-8

★ **OVER THE RIVER AND THROUGH THE WOODS by Joe DiPietro.** Nick sees both sets of his grandparents every Sunday for dinner. This is routine until he has to tell them that he's been offered a dream job in Seattle. The news doesn't sit so well. "A hilarious family comedy that is even funnier than his long running musical revue *I Love You, You're Perfect, Now Change.*" –*Back Stage* "Loaded with laughs every step of the way." –*Star-Ledger* [3M, 3W] ISBN: 0-8222-1712-0

★ **SIDE MAN by Warren Leight.** 1999 Tony Award winner. This is the story of a broken family and the decline of jazz as popular entertainment. "... a tender, deeply personal memory play about the turmoil in the family of a jazz musician as his career crumbles at the dawn of the age of rock-and-roll ..." –*The NY Times* "[SIDE MAN] is an elegy for two things – a lost world and a lost love. When the two notes sound together in harmony, it is moving and graceful ..." –*The NY Daily News* "An atmospheric memory play ... with crisp dialogue and clearly drawn characters ... reflects the passing of an era with persuasive insight ... The joy and despair of the musicians is skillfully illustrated." –*Variety* [5M, 3W] ISBN: 0-8222-1721-X

DRAMATISTS PLAY SERVICE, INC.
440 Park Avenue South, New York, NY 10016 212-683-8960 Fax 212-213-1539
postmaster@dramatists.com www.dramatists.com

NEW PLAYS

★ **CLOSER by Patrick Marber.** Winner of the 1998 Olivier Award for Best Play and the 1999 New York Drama Critics Circle Award for Best Foreign Play. Four lives intertwine over the course of four and a half years in this densely plotted, stinging look at modern love and betrayal. "CLOSER is a sad, savvy, often funny play that casts a steely, unblinking gaze at the world of relationships and lets you come to your own conclusions … CLOSER does not merely hold your attention; it burrows into you." –*New York Magazine* "A powerful, darkly funny play about the cosmic collision between the sun of love and the comet of desire." –*Newsweek Magazine* [2M, 2W] ISBN: 0-8222-1722-8

★ **THE MOST FABULOUS STORY EVER TOLD by Paul Rudnick.** A stage manager, headset and prompt book at hand, brings the house lights to half, then dark, and cues the creation of the world. Throughout the play, she's in control of everything. In other words, she's either God, or she thinks she is. "Line by line, Mr. Rudnick may be the funniest writer for the stage in the United States today … One-liners, epigrams, withering put-downs and flashing repartee: These are the candles that Mr. Rudnick lights instead of cursing the darkness … a testament to the virtues of laughing … and in laughter, there is something like the memory of Eden." –*The NY Times* "Funny it is … consistently, rapaciously, deliriously … easily the funniest play in town." –*Variety* [4M, 5W] ISBN: 0-8222-1720-1

★ **A DOLL'S HOUSE by Henrik Ibsen, adapted by Frank McGuinness.** Winner of the 1997 Tony Award for Best Revival. "New, raw, gut-twisting and gripping. Easily the hottest drama this season." –*USA Today* "Bold, brilliant and alive." –*The Wall Street Journal* "A thunderclap of an evening that takes your breath away." –*Time Magazine* [4M, 4W, 2 boys] ISBN: 0-8222-1636-1

★ **THE HERBAL BED by Peter Whelan.** The play is based on actual events which occurred in Stratford-upon-Avon in the summer of 1613, when William Shakespeare's elder daughter was publicly accused of having a sexual liaison with a married neighbor and family friend. "In his probing new play, THE HERBAL BED … Peter Whelan muses about a sidelong event in the life of Shakespeare's family and creates a finely textured tapestry of love and lies in the early 17th-century Stratford." –*The NY Times* "It is a first rate drama with interesting moral issues of truth and expediency." –*The NY Post* [5M, 3W] ISBN: 0-8222-1675-2

★ **SNAKEBIT by David Marshall Grant.** A study of modern friendship when put to the test. " … a rather smart and absorbing evening of water-cooler theater, the intimate sort of Off-Broadway experience that has you picking apart the recognizable characters long after the curtain calls." – *The NY Times* "Off-Broadway keeps on presenting us with compelling reasons for going to the theater. The latest is SNAKEBIT, David Marshall Grant's smart new comic drama about being thirtysomething and losing one's way in life." –*The NY Daily News* [3M, 1W] ISBN: 0-8222-1724-4

★ **A QUESTION OF MERCY by David Rabe.** The Obie Award-winning playwright probes the sensitive and controversial issue of doctor-assisted suicide in the age of AIDS in this poignant drama. "There are many devastating ironies in Mr. Rabe's beautifully considered, piercingly clear-eyed work …" –*The NY Times* "With unsettling candor and disturbing insight, the play arouses pity and understanding of a troubling subject … Rabe's provocative tale is an affirmation of dignity that rings clear and true." –*Variety* [6M, 1W] ISBN: 0-8222-1643-4

★ **DIMLY PERCEIVED THREATS TO THE SYSTEM by Jon Klein.** Reality and fantasy overlap with hilarious results as this unforgettable family attempts to survive the nineties. "Here's a play whose point about fractured families goes to the heart, mind – and ears." –*The Washington Post* " … an end-of-the millennium comedy about a family on the verge of a nervous breakdown … Trenchant and hilarious …" –*The Baltimore Sun* [2M, 4W] ISBN: 0-8222-1677-9

DRAMATISTS PLAY SERVICE, INC.
440 Park Avenue South, New York, NY 10016 212-683-8960 Fax 212-213-1539
postmaster@dramatists.com   www.dramatists.com

NEW PLAYS

★ **AS BEES IN HONEY DROWN by Douglas Carter Beane.** Winner of the John Gassner Playwriting Award. A hot young novelist finds the subject of his new screenplay in a New York socialite who leads him into the world of *Auntie Mame* and *Breakfast at Tiffany's*, before she takes him for a ride. "A delicious soufflé of a satire … [an] extremely entertaining fable for an age that always chooses image over substance." *–The NY Times* "… A witty assessment of one of the most active and relentless industries in a consumer society … the creation of 'hot' young things, which the media have learned to mass produce with efficiency and zeal." *–The NY Daily News* [3M, 3W, flexible casting] ISBN: 0-8222-1651-5

★ **STUPID KIDS by John C. Russell.** In rapid, highly stylized scenes, the story follows four high-school students as they make their way from first through eighth period and beyond, struggling with the fears, frustrations, and longings peculiar to youth. "In STUPID KIDS … playwright John C. Russell gets the opera of adolescence to a T … The stylized teenspeak of STUPID KIDS … suggests that Mr. Russell may have hidden a tape recorder under a desk in study hall somewhere and then scoured the tapes for good quotations … it is the kids' insular, ceaselessly churning world, a pre-adult world of Doritos and libidos, that the playwright seeks to lay bare." *–The NY Times* "STUPID KIDS [is] a sharp-edged … whoosh of teen angst and conformity anguish. It is also very funny." *–NY Newsday* [2M, 2W] ISBN: 0-8222-1698-1

★ **COLLECTED STORIES by Donald Margulies.** From Obie Award-winner Donald Margulies comes a provocative analysis of a student-teacher relationship that turns sour when the protégé becomes a rival. "With his fine ear for detail, Margulies creates an authentic, insular world, and he gives equal weight to the opposing viewpoints of two formidable characters." *–The LA Times* "This is probably Margulies' best play to date …" *–The NY Post* "… always fluid and lively, the play is thick with ideas, like a stock-pot of good stew." *–The Village Voice* [2W] ISBN: 0-8222-1640-X

★ **FREEDOMLAND by Amy Freed.** An overdue showdown between a son and his father sets off fireworks that illuminate the neurosis, rage and anxiety of one family – and of America at the turn of the millennium. "FREEDOMLAND's more obvious links are to *Buried Child* and *Bosoms and Neglect*. Freed, like Guare, is an inspired wordsmith with a gift for surreal touches in situations grounded in familiar and real territory." *–Curtain Up* [3M, 4W] ISBN: 0-8222-1719-8

★ **STOP KISS by Diana Son.** A poignant and funny play about the ways, both sudden and slow, that lives can change irrevocably. "There's so much that is vital and exciting about STOP KISS … you want to embrace this young author and cheer her onto other works … the writing on display here is funny and credible … you also will be charmed by its heartfelt characters and up-to-the-minute humor." *–The NY Daily News* "… irresistibly exciting … a sweet, sad, and enchantingly sincere play." *–The NY Times* [3M, 3W] ISBN: 0-8222-1731-7

★ **THREE DAYS OF RAIN by Richard Greenberg.** The sins of fathers and mothers make for a bittersweet elegy in this poignant and revealing drama. "… a work so perfectly judged it heralds the arrival of a major playwright … Greenberg is extraordinary." *–The NY Daily News* "Greenberg's play is filled with graceful passages that are by turns melancholy, harrowing, and often, quite funny." *–Variety* [2M, 1W] ISBN: 0-8222-1676-0

★ **THE WEIR by Conor McPherson.** In a bar in rural Ireland, the local men swap spooky stories in an attempt to impress a young woman from Dublin who recently moved into a nearby "haunted" house. However, the tables are soon turned when she spins a yarn of her own. "You shed all sense of time at this beautiful and devious new play." *–The NY Times* "Sheer theatrical magic. I have rarely been so convinced that I have just seen a modern classic. Tremendous." *–The London Daily Telegraph* [4M, 1W] ISBN: 0-8222-1706-6

DRAMATISTS PLAY SERVICE, INC.
440 Park Avenue South, New York, NY 10016 212-683-8960 Fax 212-213-1539
postmaster@dramatists.com www.dramatists.com